Michaëlle Jean

Terry Barber

MAPLE LEAF
SERIES

Michaëlle Jean is published by
Grass Roots Press, a division of Literacy Services of Canada Ltd.

PHONE 1–888–303–3213
WEBSITE www.grassrootsbooks.net

ACKNOWLEDGMENTS

We acknowledge the financial support of the Government of Canada through the Canada Book Fund (CBF) for our publishing activities.

Produced with the assistance of
the Government of Alberta, Alberta
Multimedia Development Fund.

**Government
of Alberta** ■

Editor: Dr. Pat Campbell
Image research: Dr. Pat Campbell
Book design: Lara Minja

Library and Archives Canada Cataloguing in Publication

Barber, Terry, date
    Michaëlle Jean / Terry Barber.

(Maple leaf series)
ISBN 978–1–926583–39–6

    1. Jean, Michaëlle, 1957–. 2. Governors general—Canada—
Biography. 3. Journalists—Canada—Biography. 4. Readers
for new literates. I. Title. II. Series: Barber, Terry, 1950– . Maple
leaf series.

PE1126.N43B3656 2011   428.6'2   C2011–904440–4

Printed in Canada

Contents

CANADA

The police arrest a man in Haiti.

Refugees

The man has done no wrong.
The police arrest and beat the man.
Days later, the police dump the man
outside his home.

The man lives in Haiti. A **dictator**
controls Haiti. The police work for
the dictator. The police hurt and kill
many people.

The dictator's name is Francois Duvalier.

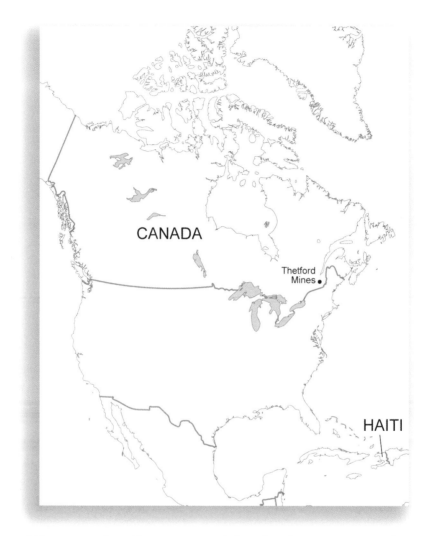

The Jean family move to Thetford Mines, Quebec.

Refugees

The man wants to be free. Two years
pass. The man **flees** to Canada in
1967. A year later, his family joins
him. The family moves to a mining
town. The family's last name is Jean.
The parent's names are Roger and
Luce.

The Jeans
come to Canada
as **refugees**.

Michaëlle Jean lives on this street.
(St. Alphonse Street)

Refugees

The Jean family is black. They live in a white town. Michaëlle is the oldest daughter. Michaëlle walks to school every day. The kids tease Michaëlle. They want to touch Michaëlle's black skin. They want to see if Michaëlle is real.

Michaëlle's younger sister is Nadege.

Michaëlle accepts all people as they are.

Hard Times

Michaëlle is real. She has lots of energy. She wants to know everything. Michaëlle loves to learn.

Michaëlle learns a hard lesson in the mining town. She learns about **racism**. But Michaëlle accepts all people as they are.

Michaëlle becomes a Canadian citizen.

Luce and her daughters live in a basement apartment.

Hard Times

There is trouble in the Jean family. Michaëlle's father is a broken man. The police beatings have changed Roger. The Jean family breaks up. Luce moves her two daughters to Montreal.

Luce works in a clothing factory.

Hard Work

Life is hard for Luce. The family is poor. Luce works hard to make ends meet. Luce works in a factory. Luce keeps her pride. Luce knows the value of education. Education gives people the freedom to make choices.

Luce also works as a nurse for 18 years.

Michaëlle gets a degree from
the University of Montreal.

Hard Work

Luce's hard work **inspires** Michaëlle. Michaëlle goes to university. She studies languages. She can speak five languages.

Michaëlle goes to university from 1979 to 1987. She also works. Michaëlle works with abused women. Michaëlle helps to open women's shelters across Canada.

Michaëlle speaks English, French, Italian, Spanish, and Haitian Creole.

Michaëlle **hosts** two TV shows.

Journalist

Michaëlle's hard work pays off.
By 1988, Michaëlle works for
Radio-Canada. She is a news reporter.
She also works for CBC Newsworld.
Michaëlle is Canada's first black
reporter on French TV.

Michaëlle Jean, Jean-Daniel Lafond,
and their daughter, Marie-Eden.

Journalist

Michaëlle likes to make films about true stories. In 1991, Michaëlle makes a film with Jean-Daniel. They fall in love and marry. In 1999, they adopt a baby from Haiti.

Michaëlle and Jean-Daniel keep making films.

Michaëlle gets French citizenship when she marries.

The Governor General represents the Queen of England.

Governor General

Michaëlle is 48. Her life changes.
Michaëlle is asked to be Canada's
Governor General. What an honour!
Michaëlle is Canada's first black
Governor General.

Michaëlle serves Canada for five years.

Michaëlle is Governor General from 2005 to 2010.

Some people think Michaëlle is a separatist.

Governor General

Most people like their new Governor General. Some do not. Some people think Michaëlle is a **separatist**. They think Michaëlle wants to break up Canada. Michaëlle says she is not a separatist.

Michaëlle gives up her French citizenship.

The Chief of Defence salutes Michaëlle Jean.

Governor General

Michaëlle is not a separatist. Michaëlle loves Canada. Canada's soldiers are special to Michaëlle. Like Michaëlle, the soldiers serve Canada.

Canada's soldiers respect Michaëlle. They would not support a separatist. The soldiers and Michaëlle form a special bond.

Michaëlle wants to listen, learn, and help.

Governor General

A Governor General reaches out to all people. Michaëlle brings people together. She asks people to share their stories. She listens to people. Michaëlle worked as a reporter. She knows how to make headlines. She knows how to make voices heard.

Michaëlle's motto is "breaking down **solitudes**."

First Nations people give Michaëlle
a Cree blanket.

Governor General

Michaëlle supports many groups.
In 2007, she meets with First Nations
women. The women are elders and
chiefs. They talk about women and
violence. Michaëlle supports women's
rights.

Michaëlle talks with young people.

Governor General

Michaëlle believes in the voice of women. She believes in the voice of youth. People feel safe with Michaëlle. People say what they think. Michaëlle listens to their concerns. She inspires people to work together and find answers.

Michaëlle looks at the "Door of No Return."

Governor General

Michaëlle goes to many places. In 2006, Michaëlle goes to Africa. She sees a sad sight. She sees the "Door of No Return." This door led to a room. The room held people who went on ships to America. They went as slaves.

The "Door of No Return" is in Senegal.

Michaëlle skins a seal.

Governor General

Michaëlle goes to Nunavut in 2009. The **Inuit** people welcome Michaëlle with open arms. She goes on a seal hunt. She helps the Inuit cut up a dead seal. An Inuit woman offers Michaëlle a piece of the seal's heart.

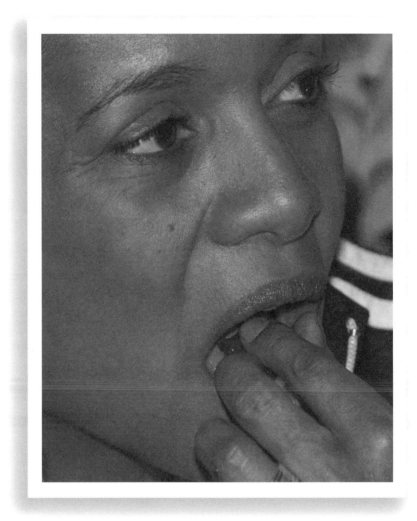

Michaëlle eats a piece of the seal heart.

Governor General

Michaëlle eats the piece of heart. She is paying respect to the Inuit people. Michaëlle accepts the Inuit for who they are. Some people think the seal hunt is wrong. They think Michaëlle should not have eaten seal meat.

Michaëlle waves goodbye.

Goodbyes

In 2010, Michaëlle's term as Governor General ends. She has won the hearts of many people. Some people want her to serve another term. But her time as Governor General is over. Michaëlle is still young. She has much to offer the world.

Michaëlle holds her mother.

Goodbyes

The next year brings **sorrow**.
Michaëlle's mother dies. Luce is 80
years old. Michaëlle sheds tears for
her mother. Luce wanted Michaëlle to
have a good life. She worked hard so
Michaëlle could have a good life.

Michaëlle speaks to school children in Haiti.

A Woman of Action

Today, Michaëlle works to make
Haiti a better place to live. Many
people in Haiti cannot read and write.
Michaëlle wants the people to have
a better education. Michaëlle knows
that education builds hope. Michaëlle
believes in the power of ideas.

Michaëlle
starts to work
for **UNESCO** in
November 2010.

Glossary

dictator: a person who rules a country in a brutal way.

flee: to run away from danger.

governor general: a person who represents the Queen in Canada.

host: to interview people on a TV show.

inspire: to encourage somebody to do something.

Inuit: Aboriginal people who live in the Arctic region.

racism: a belief that one race is superior to others.

refugee: a person who flees for safety to another country.

separatist: A Quebec separatist believes Quebec should separate from the rest of Canada.

solitude: a state of being alone.

sorrow: great sadness.

UNESCO: United Nations Educational, Scientific and Cultural Organization.

Talking About the Book

What did you learn about Michaëlle Jean?

What words would you use to describe Michaëlle?

What hardships did Michaëlle face in her life?

Describe Michaëlle's beliefs and values.

Michaëlle's motto is "breaking down solitudes." What do you think this means?

Picture Credits